Reading the News Without Losing Your Faith

Chris -
Happy Christmas
from
Anne
with love
ax

Dec. 21

Reading the News Without Losing Your Faith

Christopher R Altieri

All booklets are published
thanks to the generosity of the supporters
of the Catholic Truth Society

For E, J, R, and all the Altieris and Ritas

 First published 2021 by The Incorporated Catholic Truth Society, 42-46 Harleyford Road, London SE11 5AY. Tel: 020 7640 0042. *www.ctsbooks.org*

ISBN 978 1 78469 737 2

CONTENTS

RESTAURA CON UN FRANCOBOL
RESTORE THE COLONNADE WITH

INTRODUCTION

The Church in the Headlines

"If you don't get paid to read the Vatican pages, I'd steer well clear of them," I said to my friend, who had written to ask about the scandal *du jour*. I can't precisely recall which doctrinally dubious statement or lurid scandal my friend was exercised over, but I remember my friend's upset. This sort of thing upsets people rather easily these days. One might even suspect a significant portion of the reading public want to be put out of sorts.

'Avoid Vatican news' was strange advice from someone who makes his living by getting and writing and publishing news about the Vatican and the Church. That doesn't mean it isn't sound advice. That the Church is in a mess isn't news.

If you think it is, read the Acts of the Apostles. If you read it as any sort of "how to" manual for good governance, you're reading it wrong: the difficulties have been there from the very start. What makes my advice fundamentally misguided, however, is that it is unrealistic.

If you're a Catholic today, you will come up against reports of what's happening in the Church, including all sorts of stories about the potentially scandalous doings and sayings of churchmen. This will happen whether you are streaming news all day on your phone or a casual peruser of magazine covers and newspaper front pages. Much of what you see will be bad.

I do not mean to say only that it will be *bad* news, but also that it will be bad *news:* a large proportion of it will not really be news at all, though it may be dressed and painted as news – sometimes well enough to fool even self-styled media experts – and presented to the public as news, even though it is really editorial spin on a story that may or may not be news at all.

"The purpose of newspapers", an old saying of the business runs, "is to sell advertisements." This is true, *mutatis mutandis*, for the internet and social media age. "Sex sells," is the (very) old marketing adage, but outrage is also a close contender: current slang such as "outrage porn" gives us a clue that we may not be dealing with a generic difference so much as a special one: the outrage isn't simply to hook people in, it's the aim. Just as living in a city with healthy air and lots of green spaces is different from living in a concrete jungle perpetually enshrouded in an acrid haze, the health of the media environment influences the overall health of citizens generally. At risk from the effects of the media environment are not only those who are naive in consuming "bad" news or addicted to outrage, though they of course are the more vulnerable. Our problems are largely environmental, which means they affect all of us.

GIVE US THIS DAY OUR DAILY NEWS

In this digital age, news is produced within an artificially created twenty-four-hour "cycle" that serves markets for sensation rather than the need for publicly useful information. The news production process is driven by this cycle which starts with breaking news reports and moves through reaction, analysis, and commentary (not necessarily distinguished with adequate clarity or given in that order), and then resets with the next breaking news item. Really, it should be the other way around: news is always breaking or developing, "in real time" as we say. The twenty-four-hour news cycle, in other words, isn't a measure of the extent of time over which one cycle completes; it is an expansion of the period within which new cycles start. This is why we also live in an age of "information saturation" not entirely unlike the early age of print, in which pamphlets and tracts circulated widely for the very first time among a literate public. It took our forebears centuries to figure out how to distinguish reliable news and information outlets from unreliable ones. There's no perfect system to this day, and we're only a couple of decades into the internet age.

We're all susceptible to the baleful effects of this state of affairs. We've even developed a vocabulary for what happens to us when we get the news the way we get it these days. A few of the buzzwords are:

- Confirmation bias: the tendency we all have to believe things we either want to believe, or that fit well with our basic presuppositions about how the world is.
- Cognitive dissonance: when one person holds two or more ideas that are incompatible with each other.
- Halo effect: when one attractive attribute in a person or a product – or in our case, a story or a masthead or even an individual writer – sits over the whole thing, and puts us in a sort of thrall.
- Backfire effect: when we find ourselves presented with evidence that should cause us at least to question our basic presuppositions, but we dismiss the evidence and dig in, instead.

These phenomena are well-known and have been well studied and documented well before the dawn of the internet. They work into and out of the way we get our news in the digital age. They're built in, so to speak: a feature, not a bug, and a part of the environment. The forces at work on us in the current media environment make it harder to understand what's happening and why it matters.

Catholics are just like their fellow citizens in their susceptibility. The faith doesn't have specific remedies to cultural problems, but it *does* offer formation in ways of thinking that can help develop critical resistance to "news" whose real purpose is not information but to sell soap.

This book is one journalist's attempt to show how the cultural forces at work in our world affect the ways in which we participate in the Church's pilgrimage through this moment in history. To do that, I'll talk through some of the ways in which Catholics can draw on the resources of the faith to make sense of a world that frequently doesn't seem to be sense-making in its own right. The Church is in the world, and while we're all here, we need to get our bearings.

NCIPIS APOST PAVLVS V BVRG
VS ROMANVS PONT MAX AN

CHAPTER 1

Getting - and Keeping - Perspective

For most of Church history, most people didn't know who the Pope was. Few of them that did, cared. There were crafty popes and clumsy ones, capable popes and utter incompetents, energetic reformers and lazy time-servers, intelligent and ignorant ones, good ones and bad. Always, the institution of the papacy was more important than who wielded its power. The office, in other words, has always been more important than the officeholder. It still is, but the contemporary papacy has undergone some very significant transformations.

Even in the early days of mass media – really until well into the 20th century – popes made the papers in the society pages, when they appeared at all. This was fine for everyone involved. Or was, until it wasn't. The world got faster and smaller, and the media was literally galvanised and electrified.

THE POPE WHO TOOK TO THE AIRWAVES

Pius XI really brought the Church up to speed when he started Vatican Radio. Guglielmo Marconi himself, the father of radio, set up the operation for the Pope, and made the announcement when Pius XI first took to the airwaves. "I have the highest honour", he said, "of announcing that in only a matter of seconds the Supreme Pontiff, Pope Pius XI, will inaugurate the Radio Station of Vatican City State."

"The electric radio waves", Marconi went on to say, "will carry to all the world his words of peace and blessing." Then, Pius XI spoke – in Latin, unremarkably at the time:

> *Qui arcano Dei consilio succedimus in loco Principis Apostolorum, eorum nempe quorum doctrina et praedicatio iussu divino ad omnes gentes et ad omnem creaturam destinata est, et qui primi in loco ipso mira sane ope Marconiana uti frui possumus, ad omnia et ad omnes primo Nos convertimus atque, hic et infra Sacro Textu iuvante, dicimus: Audite caeli quae loquor, audiat terra verba oris mei. Audite haec omnes gentes, auribus percipite omnes qui habitatis orbem, simul in unum dives et pauper. Audite insulae et attendite populi de longe.*

Saying (in my translation):

> Since, by the arcane counsel of God, we succeed [we have fallen into] in the place of the Prince of the Apostles, whose doctrine and preaching by God's command is destined to all nations and to every creature (*Mt* 28:19; *Mk* 16:15), and being able for the first time to avail ourselves in this very place of the use of the marvellous Marconian work [invention], we turn in first place to all things and all people, telling them, here and below, helped by the text of Sacred Scripture: Give ear, ye islands, and hearken, ye people from afar (*Is* 49:1).

That, friends, is how it began for Vatican Radio, which carried the voice of the Holy Father into dialogue with the universal Church and with the world – really into the whole universe – and for more than a dozen years I had the great honour of serving on the English news desk there.

It was an honour. It was also a joy. I'd grown up in the 80s and 90s listening to the radio. I loved the local (New York) AM sports radio channel and the classic rock channels on FM in Connecticut, and also Garrison Keillor's edifying and delightful homespun *A Prairie Home Companion*, the banter of *Wait, Wait, Don't Tell Me!*, the level-headedness of *All Things Considered*. I'd already come to love the whole medium by the time another great radio programme premiered in 1995: Ira Glass's *This American Life*, to the podcast of which I became a devoted listener.

All but one of those programmes I just named began on the radio, and all but one – *A Prairie Home Companion* being the exception – have found a way to inhabit the digital space that permeates reality in the early 21st century. They stand out, because not many programmes born on radio have achieved similar success.

OUT WITH THE OLD, IN WITH THE NEW

Even big "old media" or "legacy media" printed publications that survived and have managed to continue as going concerns, and even to grow, have not quite found their core identity. At least, they haven't worked out how to express their core identity in a way that is intelligible and attractive. They've either become something else, or "retooled" in a way that has let them continue doing something that looks like what they used to do, but really is quite different. Church institutions are going through much the same thing, as are the churchmen who fill her offices.

Pope St John Paul II built on the work of his predecessors in the period following the Second World War, to transform the way in which the papal officeholder used the office to serve the mission of the Church. It's tough to say whether John Paul II was simply combining his gifts and talents with the powers of the office and harnessing available technology to shape the present as best he could, or implementing a considered plan for the reinvention of the office he occupied. It's easy to get embroiled in such a question – ask any two historians and you'll get eight opinions on the matter – but it doesn't really matter for our purposes. Whether by design or by accident, during the papacy of St John Paul II, people in the Church and throughout the world came to expect the Pope to be a public figure and, if not precisely a spectacle, a special attraction in ways not even dimly foreseen a generation earlier. More to the point: people – popes included – began to think of the papacy in a different way.

In fact, many people, both within the Church and without, began to think of the Pope and the papacy for the very first time. Who he was and what he was saying suddenly mattered in a way they never had before. What, exactly, the Pope's powers are – and whether a given pope is exercising them well or even appropriately – became real questions and live issues for the broad public. For the first time in history, they were questions about which one could reasonably expect the man in the street to have an opinion.

To be fair – and accurate – a good bit of this started before Pope St John Paul II was elected in 1978. A decade earlier, his predecessor, Pope St Paul VI, upset the world with a "rethinking" of the Catholic Church's teaching on contraception. From our modern, media-savvy perspective the management of the media side of that affair left much to be desired. People had false hopes raised. The Church did a poor job of both managing expectations and explaining what the debate was – and wasn't – about. Journalists covering the business had a story, and told it.

The very short version of what happened is: Pope Paul VI's encyclical, *Humanae Vitae* (on the regulation of birth) answered one outstanding question in light of established morality: are the recently developed chemical-pharmaceutical means of regulating women's fertility consistent with the natural moral order as authoritatively understood by the Catholic Church? The short answer was "No." The slightly longer answer was, "Not if they are used in order to frustrate any natural end of the sex act." Pope Paul explained his answer over several thousand words, many of them highly technical and in a philosophico-theological register that had become almost unintelligible to the broad public. That did not quell the inevitable controversy, but thereafter it seemed as if he took no further interest, letting the misunderstandings run their course.

AN UNRULY BUNCH

People had somehow got the (mistaken) impression that the Pope could change Church teaching whenever he felt like it. Yet journalists discovered that "pope considers change to Church teaching" is the kind of story that moves copy, hence, the kind that sells soap. Pope St John Paul II decided he'd give the scribblers a better story. He got on a plane, and spent the next quarter-century trotting the globe. He issued several teaching documents, offered a remarkably powerful catechetical tool to fill the gaps of Paul VI's encyclical, and *showed* people what a life of joy in the gospel looks like. It was a sight to see.

Recently, we have learned about some of Pope St John Paul II's significant failures in Church governance, and it is absolutely essential that we expose his record of leadership to the most rigorous public scrutiny. "The Church tells me that Pope John Paul II is a saint in heaven," I wrote for the *Catholic Herald* in late August of 2018. "I believe her, and I give thanks to God for the gift of his no-doubt powerful intercession." Still, I said then, we'll eventually discover that it was not because of his governance, but despite it, that Providence has thus honoured him. I stand by that. I'll add now that criticism of his leadership record in this or

that regard cannot erase what he did well – and he was an extraordinarily gifted communicator without doubt – and that's part of the problem.

Pope St John Paul II reigned so long and used available means of communication so well, that the institutions built over centuries to handle the papacy – which had a hard time adapting to the athletic young Polish man with film star good looks and a knack for improvisation – eventually caught up, and institutionalised their modes and methods of handling the "new" pope. In other words, the systems that papal handlers jury-rigged to get the most out of John Paul II were now the ones stably in place *for the Pope*, whoever he was. This had immediate practical consequences. Some of them were immediately discernible, while others took some time to recognise. All together, they were a very mixed bag.

MEET THE NEW BOSS...

Pope Benedict XVI is on record as saying he resigned the papacy in part because he wanted his successor to be in place with sufficient time for him prepare to attend the World Youth Day in 2013. Benedict judged that he would not be able to deal with the challenges, and wanted the Pope to be there, so he decided it was time he should pass on the role of pope. "With the programme set out by John Paul II for these World Youth Days," the Pope-emeritus told Elio Guerriero of Italy's *La Repubblica* in August 2016, "the physical presence of the Pope was indispensable." Benedict consulted with his medical team, and decided he was not strong enough to make the trip to Rio de Janeiro in 2013. "This, too," he said, "was a circumstance that made my resignation a duty."

"I would never be able to take part in the World Youth Day in Rio de Janeiro," Benedict told *La Repubblica*. "From that day," he said, "I had to decide in a relatively short time the date I would step down (Italian: [*D*]*ovetti decidere in un tempo relativamente breve sulla data del mio ritiro*.") Only, why? Why couldn't Pope Benedict XVI or anyone else send a legate? Why did there need to be a World Youth Day at all? Benedict's decisions are as amenable to criticism as any other pope's. Right or wrong, however, he felt that the event needed to go forward as planned, and as planned it needed the Pope. So, he needed not to be pope. That's how we got from there to here – and it also tells us that the papacy had changed in ways that made the office almost unrecognisable.

That is another very short version of a very long and complex story. It is what you get from journalism and journalists. Even when you're reading a story that runs into the many thousands of words, detailing months or years of painstaking investigation carefully reconstructed, you're getting hundreds – if not thousands – of pages of documents, dozens – if not hundreds – of hours of interviews, reduced to a few thousand words with pull-quotes (those are the "catchiest" quotes in a story, which frequently get "pulled" from the main body text and set in boldface) and a story frame (the narrative devices and techniques that journalists use to tell the stories they tell).

We journalists sometimes forget this and so do readers of the news. It's important to be mindful that no matter how neat and tidy an explanation of events is, it's always partial in the sense that it only tells a part of the story. The neater and tidier an explanation, the more closely and carefully ought readers to test the explanation's explanatory power.

KNOWING WHAT AND KNOWING HOW

Sometimes, new technology can help make this possible. Online access to local papers means stories can have a broader reach than they used to have. The internet allows news outlets to share document troves, for example, against which enterprising readers can check the journalists' work. Other journalists can mine the troves for pieces of the story that the reporters may have misconstrued or missed entirely. Other times, different journalists have very different takes on the same information.

I remember once during the reign of Benedict XVI, when *The New York Times* published a story about the then-Cardinal Joseph Ratzinger allegedly dragging his feet and first delaying, then abating, a canonical process against a priest of the Archdiocese of Milwaukee who had abused hundreds of deaf boys over a period of more than twenty years, from the 1950s to the 1970s. I won't tell you the whole story, but suffice it to say that none of the churchmen came out of it terribly well. A close reading of the documents to which the online version of the *Times*' story linked, however, showed that then-Cardinal Ratzinger's concern was primarily to see the offender declared irregular for the exercise of Holy Orders – officially suspended, in essence – without a lengthy and cumbersome (not to mention a secret) canonical process.

Who was right? Who was wrong? It isn't tough to say; it is impossible to say. In fact, they're the wrong questions. Journalists aren't supposed to answer those questions. They're supposed to tell readers what happened. The so-called "Five Ws" (Who? What? Where? When? Why?) are the basic questions news reports should answer, as fully as possible, allowing readers to make up their own minds. Anything else in a news story will be a sign that the story isn't only or entirely what it purports to be.

That business with *The New York Times* happened more than a decade ago – in 2010 – and even though I *feel* like I remember it as though it was yesterday, it really wasn't. Lots of water has flowed under the bridge since then. The polarisation of discourse in the Church has grown sharper and more intense.

It's easy to blame technology for our troubles and foolish to think we can ever escape the tendencies to which all fallen nature is prone this side of the celestial Jerusalem. There are no excuses for not being constantly vigilant.

THE COSMIC AND THE MICROCOSMIC

A few pages back, I was talking about radio. Perhaps it's because of my training in philosophy, but the cosmic power of radiophony has always been wondrous to me. The idea of energy waves nearly as ancient as time, which we can manipulate, is a captivating one. They have travelled to earth from the basement of time, and let us glimpse the slivers of slivers of seconds after the universe was born. They carry sound at the speed of light, which we terrestrial mortals can manipulate. They carry the human voice – that peculiar admixture of sound and breath, characteristic of the intelligence by which we know that God made human nature in his own image and after his own likeness – beyond the ends of the earth and into the vastness of heaven.

I'd been telling the big-small story of Vatican Radio. Suffice it to say that the new(ish) Dicastery (formerly Secretariat) for Communications, charged with the reform of the media structures of the Holy See, absorbed The Thing That Used to Be Vatican Radio, starting around 2015; precisely what is to replace it has not quite taken shape. That story is a condensed version – in microcosm – of what's been happening in the whole Church and in the world over the last several decades: we have seen the end of an era.

If this were a history book, I'd spend at least one meaty chapter on the golden age of radio, another on the advent of television, another on the mass media age from the 1950s to the 1990s; a good quarter to a third of the book – I suspect – would have to be on the period from the late 90s to the early 2000s. That's all part of the story, but things have sped up so much that past and present are right on top of one another now. Saying anything about what is and what was and what's changing into what is a delicate business and frequently a fool's errand. Instead, I'd like to key into this sense of being in a fog, and work out from wherever we are, to see whether we can't get our bearings, bit by bit.

There's another reason I liked radio for this introductory work: faith comes by hearing. God exercises his creative power by his voice. In his primordial act of creation, he speaks the being of the world. We are made in his image and after his likeness. One practical consequence of that is that our ability to say things to one another – to give our word and to keep it – is what makes us human. It's precisely our ability to have words with each other that is so much attenuated in the present.

In another book I wrote a few years ago, I talked a bit about how "to have words with somebody" means to quarrel. When people are quarrelling – especially when they are close – they need to be especially mindful of their words. Any slight misstatement could create a misunderstanding, which then risks creating disagreement where actually there is none, placing badly a genuine disagreement, or a number of other things; any of these could disrupt the dialogue or even bring it to an abrupt halt.

It goes without saying – doesn't it? – that querulousness does not naturally foster the mindfulness we need in such circumstances. The situation is rather challenging.

BETTER THAN IT SEEMS (AND ALSO WORSE)

Here are two ideas, from the core of the faith, which will help. The first is a "big picture" idea – a truth of faith, really – which is good to keep in mind. The second is some practical advice from Scripture. I'll illustrate both by examples. I suspect we'll find they have a broad range of applicability.

The first is that the Barque of Peter – the Church – will come safely to port. This is a truth of faith, which Our Lord and Saviour promised to St Peter and the Apostles while he was bodily present on Earth; it cannot fail. Our faith in this promise must be unshakable, as the rock upon which it is set – Christ, Our Lord – is unshakable. This is the dogma of the Church's indefectibility.

However, the teaching does very little in the here-and-now for people who have been raped by priests, gas-lighted by bishops, swindled by papal agents, bullied and brow-beaten by clerics, or have otherwise come in for bad treatment – some just rough, some genuinely abominable – from those appointed to bear exemplary witness to the truth of the Gospel and dispense the mysteries of salvation. It does less for people who, whether or not they know it, have a right to expect the gospel from each of us.

People are hurting. We all have a right to know what's going on – news is important – and everyone has a right to the Gospel, to the Church as Christ intends her to be – living as Christians in the world is important, too – and we need each in order to do the other, but the two things often seem designed to get in each other's way. Whether by design or by accident of providence, being in the world while not being of it requires that we be able to see clearly how bad things are, without losing sight of the good. That's the nutshell version of why it is important that we keep our heads when reading the news.

There's a line from Scripture on which I sometimes call, when I read a story that makes me angry – especially if it is a story about someone with whom I disagree, or someone I think is not doing a very good job – especially when I find that I want to be angry about the matter: *Fiant dies eius pauci, et episcopatum eius accipiat aliter*. "Let his days be few, and his bishopric another take." It's a line that stands out from Psalm 108 (109), one of the "imprecatory" or cursing psalms. The author was very angry with someone when he wrote it.

The line reminds me of the psalm, and the psalm reminds me that history is ultimately under Providence, that big shots have been mucking it up for a good long while and we're still here, and that mercy and justice are duties to which we are all called always and unconditionally. It also reminds me that there's someone out there, right now, who's praying this psalm about something I said or did – or would be, if he knew the psalm – so it calls me to an examination of conscience. It reminds me not to do the things the fellow apparently did, who came in for the cursing:

> [H]e remembered not to shew mercy, but persecuted the poor man and the beggar; and the broken in heart, to put him to death. And he loved cursing, and it shall come unto him: and he would not have blessing, and it shall be far from him. And he put on cursing, like a garment: and it went in like water into his entrails, and like oil in his bones. May it be unto him like a garment which covereth him; and like a girdle with which he is girded continually. This is the work of them who detract me before the Lord; and who speak evils against my soul. (*Ps* 108:16-22)

I think to myself, "Don't be that guy." The experience of reading a story designed to make readers upset is a little different for me: because I practise the craft of journalism, I can spot it pretty easily, and probably know what it's *really* about. I might be angry with myself for not grasping it first and writing it better. Then again, maybe I had it but decided not to do anything with it, precisely because it was the sort of thing that's good for getting rage-clicks and angry shares, but not much else. Our actions – or omissions – have consequences. "But thou, O Lord, do with me for thy name's sake: because thy mercy is sweet. Do thou deliver me, for I am poor and needy, and my heart is troubled within me." Unlike the news, Scripture is, after all, always true.

In any case, whatever you've read isn't the signal to start getting ready for the end of the world; that signal was given long ago, from a much better source than any news item will ever be able be able to boast. It probably isn't a sign that the end is at hand, either. "[T]hese things must come to pass", we read in the Holy Gospel according to St Matthew (24:6). The world has always been ending. The mess we're in is a sign it's still going, and if it is really the end, it's the thing for which "we wait in joyful hope."

Then again, it isn't so much the end that worries us, as it is the part we're told will happen right before the end; I suppose we'd all prefer not to be here for that. There's nothing we can do about it, though. Either it is now or it isn't yet, and whether it is or it isn't changes nothing about what we can and cannot – must and must not – do just now.

CHAPTER 2

What is News?

Here we are, maybe a third of the way through a book that purports to tell you how to read the news without becoming unhinged, and I still haven't said what news is.

The short answer is, whatever the editor decides is news. Though brief, this reminds us that news is a curated affair. "The news" has gatekeepers, people who decide what is news and what isn't – what's worth telling people and what isn't – and decide how much of which stories to tell you from which points-of-view. The short answer also leaves out important calculations an editor might – should – make. Does the editor have reporters who know the story and its context? Is it a story the editor's staff can turn around in time? How much explaining will a news writer have to do in order to convince readers that the story is worth their time? There are about a half-dozen things for which editors will look in a story.

HOW IMPORTANT IS IT?

The first consideration is "impact": the perceived importance of the story. Anyone who has seen a newsroom drama will recognise the shift in newsroom focus when the once-in-a-decade or once-in-a-century story breaks. Think of 9/11, or the US Capitol riots or the earthquake and subsequent tsunami that devastated north-eastern Japan in 2011. Dramas get made about those or similar fictional(ised) events because they are enormous, they make great stories because they are great – and terrible – stories. The newsroom is humming along when the "wires"[1] go bonkers or the cable news cuts to a major breaking story; suddenly all hands drop what they are doing to work on the one big story that might happen no more than once a decade.

I was teaching a class across the river from Vatican Radio headquarters on the day the news broke of Benedict XVI's resignation. The co-ordinator of the English news desk – my dear friend, Charley Collins – knew where I was and knew I had my mobile turned on but set to silent. "In case the Pope dies," I'd told him, "otherwise don't call me while I'm

---

[1] Journalists' sources of raw news material, "wire services" such as Reuters and AFP.

teaching." So, when the phone rang about five minutes into my class and I saw it was Charley calling, I answered right away. He was calling me back to the office urgently because the Pope had just resigned. I didn't quite catch the last word – I was expecting another – and was a little surprised he felt he needed to say why he was calling. "Died?!?" I asked. "Re-signed," said Charley, enunciating carefully. I briefly informed my class that we'd be wrapping up early, explained why, and answered a few questions. Then I ran across the bridge and back to the office, and into a sleepless marathon month of work.

Those are days one remembers, but most days we're picking from a big batch of smallish stories. What choices editors make depends in no small degree on the kind of publication they're editing. An affairs and commentary organisation – even one with a pretty strong news staff – won't necessarily highlight the big news stories of the day. So, the news stories you see on a magazine cover (digital or print) won't likely be breaking news reports and won't likely be reports at all in the strict sense.

YESTERDAY'S NEWS

Another thing that makes a news story is timeliness. Is it news in the basic sense that it happened recently enough to make the news pages? "Newspapers", the saying goes, "are where people read about what happened yesterday." Nowadays, fewer and fewer people get their news in printed newspapers. Even the many people who still like to sit with a broadsheet and a cup of coffee in the morning will already have read about what they read in the morning paper. The world moves faster than that.

I tell my news writers to focus on what happened in the last twelve hours. If a story is older than that, people will probably have read about it elsewhere already. If they haven't, they usually won't miss it. An editor might put a pin in a story and assign someone to write something on it in greater depth, but then it isn't a breaking news story anymore.

At other times, a story may be old in the form one encounters it, but might also have seen some development. "See if the story has moved," is something an editor or news director will say to a reporter, indicating that the reporter ought to have a look around the local papers to see what the latest on the story is. "Move the story," is another instruction editors will give: it tells a reporter or news writer to make a call and get a comment, or dig for a fact, or do something else to get the story back towards the top of the news.

BOG STANDARD/LINE STANDARD

If you're reading this and wondering whether it doesn't all sound rather manufactured, don't worry, it is. No matter how big or small the newsroom, there are always more stories than there are scribblers who can possibly do them justice. It's far from a perfect system, but then *story selection* is an art, not a science. The important thing for a news reader to know is that most organisations are working with too few resources for the job, under impossible deadline pressure.

If you're wondering why your favourite weekly or monthly publication didn't cover that *Very Important Story* about which you saw headlines in sixteen other places and read in three, it probably has far more to do with staffing and general resource management than it does with anything else – and anyway, you'd already read about it, because those other organisations got the news out first.

These days, lots of this kind of work – breaking news reporting – is still farmed out to news agencies. Journalists still call them "wire services" owing to their origins in the ancient days of telegraphy. There are several very good ones, both Catholic and secular. It is worth remembering that when an editor decides to use "wire copy" to cover a story, the reader is almost always getting the barest bones of the matter. The story is breaking and needs coverage *right now* and the editor has the wire copy to hand, so in it goes.

News agencies have different kinds of arrangements with their clients. Most are subscription-based, and most allow editors to fiddle with the copy for style and even substance. Adding a quotation to flesh out a story is quicker and easier than writing a whole new piece, and publications have their own style guides. Sometimes, an in-house news writer will rewrite a story to fit the publication's style, readership, and *editorial line*, i.e. the way in which a publication situates itself within the spectrum of opinion and across a range of issues.

These are fairly stable, but not usually written down anywhere. Readers will discern a publication's editorial line from the editorial pages. There, readers will discover whether a publication tends, for example, to be centre-left or centre-right. It's good to know the editorial line of the publications you read, but when you're reading straight news reporting it shouldn't make too much difference to the story. It *shouldn't,* yet it frequently does, as a matter of fact, affect the story.

MAKING SAUSAGE

There's something else to keep in mind. A rewrite may be very well done, but it is not original reporting. When a news writer revises another's writing, the right thing for the writer to do is usually to give a nod to the publication that broke the news, and properly acknowledge any original reporting on which the news writer relies. This does not always happen; it does not always need to happen; when it should happen, it usually does. Even when things go more-or-less as they should, however, the re-use of original reporting in brief news write-ups can contribute to confusion. Here is where the discerning reader can properly discriminate.

When news is breaking, the reporters on the ground have a big advantage. Their stories get picked up, reprinted, republished, quoted and attributed, and cited all around the world. Usually, this is fine. Occasionally, a misreported fact slips in or the story is just plain wrong. "What do you mean it's 'fake news'?!?!?" one might ask. "Multiple sources reported the story!" Ask yourself: "Did they, though?" What one often gets is multiple news outlets running their stories based on a single report – one that may be rather "thin" at least to start – thus creating a sort of echo chamber. It's the old adage about a lie oft repeated, at work. Only, it need not be an outright lie or any deliberate untruth.

Imagine that one organisation puts out a report – one with bad premises or some significant factual mistake – which others pick up. This happens with popes more frequently than it does with other figures, owing to the global interest, multilingual press corps, and chronic shortage of good religion reporters and editors in newsrooms around the world. It happens more frequently with Pope Francis than with his predecessors, owing to the reigning pontiff's penchant for speaking off the cuff and improvising away from the prepared script. Two examples from early on in his pontificate will illustrate the point.

In October 2014, Pope Francis gave a speech to participants in the plenary assembly of the Pontifical Academy of Sciences, gathered in the Vatican to discuss "Evolving Concepts of Nature" especially insofar as the origins of human being were concerned. "God", one widely distributed news service reported Francis as saying, "is *not a divine being* or a magician, but the Creator who brought everything to life." A fracas followed.

The pro-Francis elements in the commentariat did some impressive gymnastics to explain what Francis 'clearly' meant by the unusual turn-of-phrase, while the rabidly anti-Francis crowd took the expression as proof positive that the Socialist-Jesuit-Freemason Axis had infiltrated the Vatican and seized the papacy. The problem lies deeper, though: Francis never said the thing they all said he said. What Francis said was, "God is not a demiurge or a magician, but the Creator who gives life to all beings." Who knows whether a harried reporter decided "demiurge" was too abstruse a term for average readers and a distracted editor let it through, or whether a diligent reporter was let down by an editor with too low an esteem of readers' theological vocabularies and too little regard for the beat reporter's expertise. Regardless, the damage was done.

A little over a year later, on 19th November 2015, Pope Francis said morning Mass in the chapel of the *Domus Sanctae Marthae* in the Vatican. He gave one of his brief homilies – really they're more in the vein of the *fervorino*, frequently insightful though rarely models of clarity – in which he was reported to have said that Christmas was a sham (or a charade, or a scam). People were outraged at his appalling language. Again, commentators rushed in to explain what he *really* meant. Again, he hadn't said the thing they said he'd said.

"Today", Pope Francis really said, "Jesus is in heaven: he watches us," and "he will come to us on the altar." "Jesus weeps even today", Pope Francis went on to say, "because we have preferred the way of war, the way of hate, the way of enmity." He took some homiletic liberty and sacrificed some rigour of theological precision with his line about Jesus weeping, and no one would accuse him of stirring oratory on the occasion, but there's nothing close to appalling or unusual there. He went on to say that we could see more clearly what he was talking about if we considered that "we are close to Christmas: [when] there will be lights, festivities, luminous trees, even crèches, everything decked out – [but/while] the world continues to make war, to wage wars."

If you're wondering how anyone got "Christmas is a sham" in quotes from that, the answer is easy. The Italian expression for "everything decked out" is *tutto truccato*. Now, the Italian verb, *truccare*, has a wide array of possible meanings: it could refer to putting on cosmetics – *trucchi* – or it could refer to a "trick" – *trucco* – or even "rigging" a game of chance – "loaded dice" are *dadi truccati* – or a sporting match. In short, a translator got it wrong – took *truccato* in the sense of "sham" – and other news writers followed, while editors didn't know or didn't care to stop and check against the original. It was a relatively small slip that turned into clickbait and outrage.

FIT TO PRINT?

"News" is, therefore, anything new and/or current, with relatively significant public import or interest – real or perceived – or sufficiently out of the ordinary to merit mention (one thinks of the "man bites dog" variety of news story). There are two other common types of stories: those that either chronicle conflict or drive controversy, and those involving the private lives of public figures.

The private affairs of public figures can be tricky, because public figures do not enjoy rights to privacy in exactly the same way that private men and women enjoy them. Celebrities are one thing – they're frequently well-known for being well-known, and really are better left alone (if you ask me) – but when they use their notoriety to champion public causes, they become fair game. People in positions of public trust are obliged to put up with attenuated privacy rights, precisely because their character and conduct does matter to the public.

It was news when General Petraeus had an affair with his official biographer a few years ago, because it is a crime under the military code for officers to engage in extra-marital affairs, and that sort of behaviour is criminal for officers because it is a security risk. Similarly, Pope Francis's decision to give Mgr Battista Ricca (the fellow about whom Pope Francis made his now-famous "Who am I to judge?" remark) a sensitive position inside the Institute for the Works of Religion despite his track record of questionable "private" behaviour should have raised more eyebrows than it did for that reason.

In the Church, however, the public debate turned on whether the Pope was somehow condoning his private behaviour. The real story, it seems to me, was that Francis apparently trusted Mgr Ricca – a trust the Holy Father confessed was based on limited personal acquaintance and the fact that Ricca was never found guilty of any crime – despite the distrust of Ricca's former superior, the Apostolic Nuncio to Uruguay.

The short version of the story, as Sandro Magister of Italy's *L'Espresso* told it, is that Ricca came to Uruguay from Bern, accompanied by a fellow – an officer in the Swiss army, it happens – with whom he apparently had a particular friendship and for whom he wanted a job in the nunciature. The nuncio prevented that, but retired shortly after Ricca arrived, and then Ricca – who was *chargé d'affaires* at that point – appointed his friend to the job.

If that wasn't enough, there were also reports of his being beaten one night either during or after a visit – one of many, despite warnings – to one of Montevideo's homosexual cruising venues. On another occasion, he got stuck in a lift with another passenger, and needed rescue. The police came, and found him in the company of a young fellow known to the police.

So, there were concerns over what I described for the *Catholic World Report* as "serial ambiguities in Ricca's personal moral conduct."

I'd say it is fair to consider a fellow with that sort of reputation a potential security risk, too, quite apart from his "personal" moral struggles. As I noted for *Catholic World Report*, Pope Francis wasn't wrong when he said, "If someone is gay and is searching for the Lord and has good will, then who am I to judge him?" The thing is, the pope was not discussing a judicial judgement. He was responding to a question regarding a personnel decision he had made. It's fair to note – as I did for *Catholic World Report* – that Pope Francis also said he ordered a preliminary investigation. "From this investigation," he said, "there was nothing of what had been alleged. We did not find anything of that." This all transpired in or about 2013. We've since learned more about "preliminary investigations" in the Church – about what they're worth and what they're not – and they're not always or even very frequently worth very much. Live and learn, I suppose.

What would happen to the climate and tenor of discourse in the Church if we all started thinking about things in such and similar terms, rather than taking everything as fodder for the scandal sheets?

SELLING THE NEWS

Reporters and editors and headline-writers know that they need to move copy. Why does scandal sell? "Human nature" is a fair answer, but *what* is the real scandal in any given story? That's a question all of us should be asking regularly – journalists and readers alike – each in his or her own way.

Nobody should want the worst to be true – not ever, not about anyone or anything – but sometimes it is. Sometimes, the truth is worse than we have imagined it might be. "It is hard to confront horrible things and seek out the truth," I wrote in an August 2018 piece for the *Catholic Herald* purporting to get at "The Root of the Abuse Crisis" in the Church, "while not being fully convicted of the worst until one has all the evidence necessary to support the conviction." It is hard – it's hard to do as a journalist and it is hard to do as a reader.

"Nevertheless", I went on to say, "that is precisely what the bishops failed to do, with disastrous consequences. The full truth might be harder still, but it must out." Whether the truth that must out regards politicians or prelates or other powerful people, one thing is absolutely essential: that none of us be quick to blame the people on the other side of the issue – whatever it is – or be too willing to give "our" guys – whoever they are – a pass. The temptation to do both is always there, and it will always prove fatal to reform efforts. This is especially true when it comes to the Church, but it is true not only for ecclesiastical reform.

When it comes to public controversies it's also important to distinguish *reports* on current controversies, from "side-taking" on the issue. It's one thing to give the main lines of this-or-that public issue, along with statements from leading figures on the different sides of the issue and some rehearsal of the reasons for which the business touches the common weal. It's quite another to prefer one side of a publicly disputed question over another. It's quite another matter still to present one side of an issue or one view on a question as though it were the right side or the right take – or even the only side or the only take, which is to say: as *news* reporting, rather than commentary or editorial positioning.

Regarding prominent people and their affairs, there are two things to consider. One is the reason their business – whatever its specifics – finds itself before the public. The other is the kind of interest the story may have for the public, regardless of popular curiosity. *Nota bene*: these are different – sometimes very different – considerations. The former encompasses the possible motives of those who have made the facts or assertions that form the basis of the story known to the public. The latter wonders whether there is a real public interest beyond or apart from natural public curiosity. There is frequently some significant overlap in the answers, but none is necessary.

WHEN THE WHEELS COME OFF THE BUS

It's important as well that one be able to distinguish the two kinds or levels of consideration. A fairly recent controversy in the Church will illustrate why: *L'Affaire Viganò*. Here is a brief refresher of the bones of the business (more or less as I rehearsed it in a preliminary analysis piece, again for the *Catholic World Report*):

- Archbishop Carlo Maria Viganò, who had a long career in the Secretariat of State and eventually served as Apostolic Nuncio to the United States from 2011-2015, published a letter in late August 2018 – the release of the missive was a carefully orchestrated affair, timed to coincide with Pope Francis's return from Ireland after the World Meeting of Families – alleging systematic cover-up of the disordered and abusive behaviour of the former Archbishop of Washington, then-Cardinal Theodore Edgar "Uncle Ted" McCarrick, who had resigned from the College of Cardinals and was at the time of the letter's publication awaiting canonical trial on charges he had sexually molested at least one minor. Other victims would come forward.
- It was already clear that McCarrick's behaviour was an open secret, though high-ranking prelates close to Uncle

Ted continued to claim they knew nothing. Some even said they had been unaware of any hint of impropriety.

- Archbishop Viganò's first letter sought to give the lie to all that, by detailing a nearly two-decade cover-up of McCarrick's misconduct that involved three popes and three Secretaries of State, at least a half-dozen other high-ranking Vatican officials, and several other figures.

The ink spilt over summer 2018's celebrity cleric and his "testimonies" in the three years since he published the first of them has been prodigious. Catholics who pay attention to Church news tended quickly to form opinions regarding the curial lifer and *former* papal diplomat: for some, he was – is – a paladin who charged into the fray, heedless of his personal safety, careful only of the good of the Church and the safety of Christ's faithful; for others, he was – is – a low-level con-man with a self-serving agenda and scores to settle, who saw his chance to seize a quarter-hour in the sun.

What one thought of him – or his motives for making his original claims public, or the timing of his decision to publish them – was and remains largely beside the point, if not wholly irrelevant. His main contribution, such as it was, he gave in his first spectacular *J'accuse!* published in late August 2018.

The testimony Archbishop Viganò offered was not perfectly crafted. It was not impervious to criticism. I wrote about it in the *Catholic World Report*, offering a preliminary analysis that – I think, anyway – holds up pretty well. I faulted that first letter from Viganò for the haste with which it presumed to know – with a great degree of certainty – the motives of the figures whose behaviour he denounced. That first letter also engaged in poorly-founded speculation on some very weighty matters, indeed. It was intemperate on occasion. It named several churchmen – some of them very senior – at whose roles in the McCarrick business he could but guess. Some of those men he accused of grave moral turpitude, but offered precious little in the way of explanation as to why their moral failures – real or supposed – should have any specific pertinence to the affairs that were his principal object. That sort of thing skates close to slander. I wrote a commentary piece for *The Catholic Thing* in September 2018, in which I compared him to the American underworld figure Joe Valachi:

> As far as whistle-blowers go, it is fair to think that Viganò more closely resembles the gangster-turned-federal-witness, Joe Valachi, than he does the heroic NYPD detective, Frank Serpico. A frank estimation must conclude that many of Viganò's specific allegations are either tangential, or ancillary, or simply tainted with some desire for personal vendetta.
>
> Nevertheless, as far as Archbishop Viganò's testimony is concerned, there is one central question regarding Pope Francis: is Viganò's report of his 23rd June 2013 conversation with the Holy Father accurate?

> If Viganò's recollection is not accurate, then he could be a living saint, and it would make no difference: he would still have done immense injustice to the person of the Holy Father and damage to the Office of Peter, not to mention incalculable harm to the faith of God's holy people.
>
> If Viganò's recollection is accurate, then he could be the devil himself, and it would make no difference: Pope Francis would have had a report of McCarrick's depraved character, which he should have taken seriously, and yet failed to act (*The Catholic Thing*, 14th September 2018).

One of the figures who rightly came in for a good deal of scrutiny was Uncle Ted's successor in the US capital see, Cardinal Donald Wuerl. There was, in that first letter, a titbit that jumped off the page and into my head.

Archbishop Viganò claimed that Pope Benedict XVI had put McCarrick under some sort of restriction after some word of his character and proclivities had reached the pontiff. In that first letter, Viganò overstated the nature and extent of the restrictions, but the core and substance of his claim withstood scrutiny and were eventually vindicated by the Vatican's own McCarrick Report. At the time, it was a major point of contention. That's where Cardinal Wuerl comes in.

Although Cardinal Wuerl had repeatedly denied any knowledge of the behaviour about which rumour had swirled for decades, and even abjured hearing so much as a whisper, he cancelled an event for prospective seminarians – at Archbishop Viganò's behest – which had been advertised in the archdiocesan magazine with McCarrick as the headline guest. Now, archbishops – especially cardinal archbishops of metropolitan sees – don't just roll over for bureaucrats, even ones with "Apostolic Nuncio" stencilled on the office door. If Wuerl really had no inkling of McCarrick's depravity – and more importantly, no knowledge of the alleged papal restrictions on McCarrick's public activity – it struck me as highly unlikely he would have cancelled the vocation promotion event just because the nuncio said so, no questions asked. So, I dug into it for the *Catholic Herald*, and got the Archdiocese of Washington to confirm for the *Herald* that the event had been cancelled "at the nuncio's request" even though Cardinal Wuerl "did not receive any documentation or information during his time in Washington regarding any actions taken against Archbishop McCarrick." It was one of those things that make a reporter go, "Hmmm."

WHAT MAKES NEWS?

It was a strange time, to be sure. I mention the affair to illustrate that journalists – in this case one-and-the-same journalist – can report news, offer analysis, and comment on affairs – but the journalist needs to be clear about which he or she is doing at any given time. Readers need to be able to distinguish one kind of news material from the others. Here are the three broad categories, in a nutshell:

- Reporting: when a journalist – a reporter – collects and ascertains the pertinent facts of a story, organises them, and presents them to readers succinctly. The "Five Ws" – Who? What? Where? When? Why? – are the corner, cap, and key of reporting.
- Analysis: when a reporter has an established by-line and a specific "beat" – i.e. an area of life with which the reporter is familiar and highly practised – the reporter may offer discussion of situational dynamics, trends, forces, personalities, etc. This is "News Analysis" or "Affairs Analysis". It is not "straight" reporting, but it does help readers understand, for example, how and why certain stories are important. Sometimes, a reporter writing as an analyst will include some original quotes – "So-and-so told me, '[Interesting thing XYZ]' – but those generally only illuminate what is known to the record already.
- Commentary: contrary to popular belief, commentary is not quite the same as opinion. One writing commentary will usually have some pertinent expertise, or attachment to an issue or area of interest, knowledge of events and/or players in a subject area, or a combination of these. Commentary is neither reporting nor analysis. Commentary offers informed – though often partial – "takes" on issues and affairs. Commentary will often include rehearsal of pertinent fact, but will quite deliberately avoid original reporting, and will only

incidentally include news analysis. Commentary is the most "subjective" of the three divisions.

Knowing which one is writing is a key to doing good journalism. It's of paramount importance that readers know the ones from the others and be able to identify which they're reading at any given moment. Our failure to be mindful of these distinctions – journalists' and readers' failures – exacerbates the problems.

"If one judges more broadly", I wrote for the *Catholic World Report* in August of 2019, on the first anniversary of Archbishop Viganò's first (in)famous letter, "by the substance and tenor of the public debate in the Church, we are seeing the worst ecclesiastical leadership crisis in at least five hundred years play out as a popularity contest, a war of personalities, with the impossibly puerile shorthand that comes with such fare: 'Team Francis' and 'Team Viganò.'"

"This is insane," I concluded. It was. It is. It will continue to be insane for as long as we let it be, and it will only get worse for as long as we let it.

ESIVS·ROMA

CHAPTER 3

Knowing What You Know (and What You Don't)

Anyone who wants to read the news without becoming unhinged needs to learn certain practices of mindfulness – the Old School disciplines of thought, not the New Age claptrap – especially regarding the reasons for which news and affairs publications are giving space to one story rather than another, and why they are covering a given story in the way they're covering it.

Here, the truths of the faith can help. Whenever you see something claiming the Pope is a heretic, for example, know that you are almost certainly dealing with conspiracy theory. We have it on good authority that the Barque of Peter will come safely to port. We know much less about what condition she will be in when she does arrive.

TRUTH-TELLING

News media at their best tell you what's happening on the boat and in the seas she's on. Captains can make bad decisions that lose passengers, crew and cargo, even if they aren't going to cause the ship to founder. So, if you read a story about how the Pope is not the Pope, your best bet is to read something else. There may well be a story to read and know about, but you're almost certainly safer getting the story from someone else.

You might call this test the Pevensie Protocol. Many of you will be familiar with the episode in *The Lion, the Witch, and the Wardrobe*, in which the older Pevensie children, Peter and Susan, encounter Professor Kirke and speak to him about their younger sister, Lucy, who claimed to have found a secret gateway to another world. Their younger brother, Edmund, had been giving Lucy a hard time about it. Lucy seemed quite convinced of her story, and the older children were worried about her.

"There are only three possibilities", the professor tells Peter and Susan. "Either your sister [Lucy] is telling lies, or she is mad, or she is telling the truth." There are usually lots of other possibilities in real life, including that someone may be giving a truthful account that does not agree with the facts. "You know she doesn't tell lies and it is obvious that she is not mad", the professor goes on to say. "For the moment then and unless any further evidence turns up", he concludes, "we must assume that she is telling the truth."

News reporters are the people who get paid not to make those assumptions, but to press them, and to discover – insofar as it is possible to discover them – the facts that will clarify the business. Readers are the people who need to judge the issue. In this, the bit that too frequently gets left out is the second thing that Professor Kirke mentions: "It is obvious that she is not mad." For one thing, people suffering madness frequently tell the truth. They really are seeing the things they say they see. That's why we say they're mad.

FAKE NEWS?

Pope Francis had some very interesting things to say about the fourth estate[2] in his Message for the 52nd World Day for Social Communications in 2018. The theme of the Pope's Message was from the Gospel according to St John: "The truth will set you free." The subtitle: "fake news and journalism for peace." I wrote a pretty lengthy treatment of the Message for the *Catholic World Report*, the gist of which is worth revisiting.

"Francis", I noted, "often quotes Scripture antiphonally." I meant that he will quote a line or short passage, intending to bring the broader passage to the fore of the reader's or hearer's mind. That's what antiphons do. I said that there

---

[2] Term for the profession of journalism.

was evidence the Message was one of the cases in which he was doing just that. I hedged a little bit on that claim, for modesty's sake, but I was pretty confident. Not to toot my own horn, but I've been doing this for a good while, and have developed a "feel" for these sorts of things. Journalists who have spent a good deal of time on a given "beat" will develop such sensitivities – and readers of their copy will notice, if they know what to look for.

Readers will be able to discern whether and to what extent a writer really knows his or her subject, by noticing the kinds of things a writer notices and the way in which a writer notices the things he or she does. It's not a question of agreeing or disagreeing with the writer's take, mind you. It's a matter of probing whether a writer knows what he or she is talking about. Writers will frequently expound on subjects about which they haven't the requisite expertise, simply because they've received an assignment, need to meet a deadline, and want to make sure their readers feel they've got their money's worth.

Writers of affairs commentary, especially, will frequently write with more confidence than their knowledge of their subject warrants. That's not to say they're wrong – they may well be dead-on right – but "I don't get writer's block", an old journalists' expression goes, "I get hunger pains." That is to say, writers will frequently give the reading public what the reading public wants to get, because writers want to get paid so they can eat. Indeed, the best writers will do this reliably.

It's why they are able to make a living at writing. The really good ones will give you what you need, in a way you like – or don't mind – having it. Like children and vegetables (or medicine) a little salt (or sugar) helps things go down.

"You shall know the truth", are the words Our Lord says right before he says, "the truth will set you free." In the Message, the Holy Father asks how we are to discern the truth in a climate of intolerance and hypersensitivity, both of which flourish in environs of "instantaneous emotions like anxiety, contempt, anger and frustration." He is right to pose the question, and insightful in framing it as he does.

SELLING (MORE) SOAP

Anxiety is a pretty normal human emotion. We all feel it. Some people feel more of it more keenly than the rest of us, others more constantly than others. Some people feel anxious pretty much all the time. I was about to say they feel anxious all the time about everything, but that's not quite right. People who suffer anxiety as a psychological condition are not necessarily anxious about anything in particular. They're just anxious – and their anxiety will go out in search of an object in reality on which to seize. If you suffer anxiety, or know someone who does, you won't need to hear me or anyone else say anything about how unhelpful our media environment is in these regards.

The media environment in which we live is one built to make us all more anxious – or at least differently so – than we would be, were we living without "the innerwebz" (as a former colleague delightfully referred to it). Anxious people frequently have little sales resistance when it comes to things touted as remedies or relief. When the things purporting to offer remedy or relief actually increase anxiety in the long term, by confirming the need for the thing in the first place, a vicious cycle is born and the purveyors of the product have a customer for life.

The advertising executives – "Mad Men" of Madison Avenue and their ilk – have known this for decades, but these days, there's another wrinkle. In an age of "free" news on the internet, anxious readers are not only easy targets for spivs. They – we – are the products being sold. Data miners track what we read, what we search for, what we buy. They track where we go and who we see. They know what we eat. Our phones know when we're awake and when we're asleep. Our digital devices turn our lives into series of ones and zeros, and then the owners of the hardware and software that do the collecting sell the data.

In order to survive, news outlets have got to sell advertising. Data help ad-placement firms present users with special offers on products they – we – want to buy. So, businesses collect and track and sell users' data to other businesses. Websites want readers to stay, so they use similar software to show users more of what they like to read. Click on a story about something very rare and very scary – like meningitis in children – and the next time you open

Google News, I bet there will be another story about that or something similar. Pretty soon, you'll have the idea that every third kid is sick with the disease. Really, one is more likely to be struck by lightning in one's own living room on a clear day.

It's small wonder more of us aren't more anxious than we are. Or are we? It's tough on a good day to draw the line between anxiety as an emotion and anxiety as a disordered psychological condition. The other states Pope Francis mentioned in his World Communications Day address – contempt, anger, and frustration – may all arise naturally, too. They build over time, are often rooted in some legitimate complaint, and come to the surface – when they do – because of rough or unfair treatment we or others in whom we are somehow invested have experienced.

Nevertheless, a good many of us often adopt postures of contempt in public and private discourse. One used to hear it said that we don't talk to each other in real life the way we talk to each other on social media. These days, I wonder whether that's as true as it used to be. We like to read writers who do angry well. We watch talking heads on TV who make sport of the people supposed to be their interlocutors. As long as we keep buying (or using) what they're selling (or offering), they'll keep putting it out there. The only long-term solution to this part of the problem – the only way to change the environment – is to change what's on offer. We can't do that *and* keep buying the same old goods. In general, we're pretty willing to be angry and frustrated.

If I were a spiritual advisor rather than a newsman, I might tell you here about how the way we consume news is of a piece with the way we consume other things. The tools we use to avoid unhealthy attachments to food or sex or money, or break unhealthy habits when we've formed them in those and other regards can serve us all when it comes to the news and media consumption in general.

"Fasting" from digital media is something about which there's been a good deal of talk lately (and for a good while, now), and it's a good idea, if you can do it. "Just turn it off," isn't necessarily great advice, though, even when it is theoretically practicable. It isn't necessarily practicable, either. "Just don't eat", isn't very good advice, either.

Dietology has developed a good deal, and there are nutritionists and dietologists – trained medical professionals – who can tailor a diet to your needs and goals, whether they are to lose weight, break bad habits, or just stay healthy. Some of us can eat whole bags of marshmallows at a sitting without gaining an ounce, while others (ahem) can't have an extra half-helping of Brussels sprouts without tipping the scales. Some of us are built for speed, others of us built for comfort. Some of us need 4,000 calories per day, just to break even, and how one gets them doesn't matter much. Most of us don't. It's the same, *mutatis mutandis*, for media in general and news in particular.

WHAT IS TRUTH?

"We can recognise the truth of statements from their fruits", Pope Francis went on to say, "whether they provoke quarrels, foment division, encourage resignation; or, on the other hand, they promote informed and mature reflection leading to constructive dialogue and fruitful results." I'm not sure we can.

"One may as well provoke a quarrel with a truth as with a falsehood", I noted in the treatment of the "fake news" Message from Pope Francis. One may also force an issue with a frank statement of truth, or push someone out of the conversation. We can misuse true statements, just as we can misuse the power of speech by telling falsehoods. The devil can quote Scripture. We have it on sound authority that he has, and does.

More to the point: the fact that a statement provokes a quarrel or foments division or causes discouragement is no measure of the statement's truth. "Sometimes," I noted in the same piece, "the Emperor has no clothes." Here's more:

> Our Lord said things about his coming: that it was not to bring peace but division; to set father against son and son against father; to set the whole world ablaze (cf. *Lk* 12:49-53). Such expressions are easily manipulated, and perhaps difficult to parse, or at least to apply to concrete situations. Nevertheless, they are at bottom an expression of the basic opposition Christ's coming into the world

> establishes between him and his followers, on the one side, and those surrendered to the world's addictions, on the other – hence, a warning about the inevitability of conflict, for which Christians are to be prepared.
>
> There will always be those, who respond to truth with querulousness, accuse truth-tellers of divisiveness, and receive frankness as though it were offered to discourage. The certain presence of such pathologies of responsiveness must mean that they can never serve as criteria for determining the truth of their occasions.

"An impeccable argument", Pope Francis wrote, "can indeed rest on undeniable facts, but if it is used to hurt another and to discredit that person in the eyes of others, however correct it may appear, it is not truthful." There's a good deal of truth to that. Why we say what we say is as important as what we say and when we say it.

Still, a sound argument deployed to advance a less-than-praiseworthy end is a sound argument. Solid facts often hurt feelings when they're unpleasant. Unflattering facts hurt reputations when they're widely shared. Those are both matters that regard the use we make of facts and arguments.

When it comes to public figures, especially those in offices of public trust, information regarding their character and conduct may well merit public scrutiny, precisely because it will damage their reputation. "While we hope that journalists will be careful and discriminating in these regards", I wrote, "there can be no question of their primary duty, which is to what we used to call the public weal, in the service of which it is from time to time necessary to expose the badness of powerful persons."

Pope Francis was certainly correct to say, "[A] weighty responsibility rests on the shoulders of those whose job is to provide information, namely journalists, the protectors of news." Journalists have a "duty of care" towards the reputations of the people about whom they report. They also have a duty to the public. The public trust is the foundation and reason for the journalistic profession.

NEITHER FEAR NOR FAVOUR

In other words, the standard Pope Francis proposed will always tend to favour powerful people over the little guys. That makes it problematic, to say the least. John Adams once famously said the people have:

> [the] right, from the frame of their nature, to knowledge, as their great Creator, who does nothing in vain, has given them understandings, and a desire to know; but besides this, they have a right, an indisputable, unalienable, indefeasible, divine right to that most dreaded and envied kind of knowledge, I mean, of the characters and conduct of their rulers.

Journalists inform the public. Their job is to bring facts before the citizenry as fully as possible, and to explain them as best they can. Journalists have a responsibility to frame issues fairly. They're not supposed to show favour. "Fake news is fake," I wrote in the treatment for the *Catholic World Report*, but also noted that bad press is often the result of very good journalism.

Later in the Message, Pope Francis talked about the "snake-tactics" that are "used by those who disguise themselves in order to strike at any time and place", and said that "we" – by which I took him to mean citizens and journalists together – have a duty to unmask them.

That's true, at least sometimes. If, by "unmasking" he meant something like knowing how to spot fake news, then – yes – we ought to be trained up and on the lookout for it. There's no fool-proof system or checklist for spotting fake news, but getting your news from reputable sources is one thing we can all do. Just note that "reputable" doesn't mean "in line with my worldview" or anything close.

Also, keep in mind that general news outlets like newspapers and magazines will often be better at letting you know there is a story than they will be at getting all the fine points of it exactly right. They're frequently good on the gist of things, but the devil is in the detail. When it comes to stories on a specialised beat – religion, say, or science – it's good practice to take stories you see in the dailies and weeklies (and monthlies, ahem) with a grain of salt. There's always more to the story when there is one, and sometimes the story isn't really there – not because the story is made up or twisted into something it's not – because the story is either thin or old or not really that big a deal to begin with, or a combination of all of those.

If, however, journalists and citizens were to make unmasking irresponsible or malicious media types anything like their primary concern, it would soon become their only concern. There would be little time for anything else, and less energy. Pope Francis has given better advice elsewhere, when it comes to dealing with the serpent: ignore him – and when that is impossible, rely on God. "Do not argue with Satan," Pope Francis told the faithful gathered in St Peter's Square to pray the *Angelus* with him on Sunday 9th March 2014. It wasn't the first time he'd given that advice, and would not be the last.

I talked a little earlier about the so-called "Five Ws" – Who? What? Where? When? Why? – which journalists bring the public in their news reportage. That last one is the synthesis of the first four, and – if it isn't the toughest to nail down, as I've sometimes thought and said it is – it's certainly the most open to debate.

Together, they form the basis of the public trust that journalism exists to safeguard. They constitute the substance that the ethical code by which journalists are supposed to live their professional lives exists to protect and ensure. That ethical code developed during the age of print. Commitment to journalistic practice informed by that code continued to drive the best journalism through the mass media age of radio and television. It may be that technological developments have affected our culture so deeply and so generally as to require that we ask whether journalism thus conceived and practised is still possible. If the question needs asking, the answer needs trying.

The only way to get the answer is to practise good journalistic fundamentals and see what happens. The public discourse may prove to be unsalvageable – too far gone – but the effort can't hurt. It might not save the public square, but it will help foster an environment in which the only kind of public discourse worth conducting may stand half a chance. Here are two things we can all do:

- Work against our willingness to be sold on narratives that harmonise with our general outlook and basic worldview, or show our preferred figures – whether politicians, churchmen or others – in a sympathetic light.

- Make serious, sustained, and concerted efforts to expose to unsparing criticism those ideas and views with which we agree.

Together, these two things will help us all develop the habit of "thinking all the good we can" about our fellows – especially those with whom we happen to disagree, even on very weighty matters. They will also make us better at thinking well of those others. If they don't, they'll at least help us attenuate our willingness to think the worst about the people who don't see things our way.

When the matter at hand is not opinion but behaviour, things are somewhat more tricky. CS Lewis's character Mark Studdock from *That Hideous Strength* is instructive in this regard. "This", writes Lewis of a bad thing the ambitious young academic resolved to do in order to advance himself, "was the first thing Mark had been asked to do which he himself, before he did it, clearly knew to be criminal." Lewis goes on to say:

> the moment of his consent almost escaped his notice; certainly, there was no struggle, no sense of turning a corner. There may have been a time in the world's history when such moments fully revealed their gravity, with witches prophesying on a blasted heath or visible Rubicons to be crossed. But, for him, it all slipped past in a chatter of laughter, of that intimate laughter between fellow professionals, which of all earthly powers is strongest to make men do very bad things before they are yet, individually, very bad men.

The reporter is not concerned with judging the moral character of the persons on whose actions he reports. The reporter is not strictly concerned, *qua* reporting, with the moral quality of the actions themselves. He is concerned with saying what happened, who did it, when, where, and – insofar as possible – why. "Because they are wicked men who harbour hatred of the faith and contempt for the People of God," may well be an answer to that last, especially.

Nevertheless, it is not the reporter's job to give it. It is not the reader's job to reach it, either.

If that appears to clash with my insistence on the right of the people to knowledge of the character and conduct of their rulers – including their rulers in the faith – then I can only urge that the two assertions are rather in tension with one another. It happens with a fair degree of frequency in life, that we either suspend judgement of a moral agent or allow personal knowledge or knowledge of circumstance – or both, along with other factors as well – to mitigate our judgement of an action or an actor. Then there is occasional warrant for such net judgements.

If you find yourself in search of reasons to justify or support such judgements, rather than to save the persons you are called to judge, the chances are you've lost your way. Your counsels may be poisoned. Knowing what's going on in the world and in the Church is important. Indulging an appetite for scandal is unhealthy. If you find yourself attracted to the sorts of outlets that appeal to your desire for scandal and outrage, you might consider putting them all down for at least a while.

The work of thinking all the good we can is work we all need to be doing together – all of us, including all of us Catholics – and it's just no good to say, "What about the other person?" This is the sort of work that "takes a village" but it is also the sort of work that starts with each of us. So, any time you come across a news report or commentary piece telling you to be angry and then giving you a reason, interrogate the reasons and ask yourself why you're getting this person's take. That's how you start.

One practical upshot of this: Catholics everywhere – old and young, women and men, professionals, tradesmen, lay people, clerics, religious – have an opportunity to show their fellows that Catholic religion, contrary to increasingly diffuse public opinion, is actually good for the body politic ...if the people who profess it also practise it sincerely.

Christmas is meeting with Jesus, says Pope
Cardinal wins apology for fake abuse story
News of the World apologises for slur on Catholic leader
Pope: media version of Council caused miser
In an address to priests Benedict XVI says media distortion of Vatican II led to 'calamities' but its true meaning is starting to em
Archbishop confronts BBC's anti-Church bias
'Catholics are fed up with the BBC using the licence fee to broadcast hostile and biased programmes' The Archbishop of Birmingham
'We must not miss this chance to help the BBC rid itself of a bigotry that belongs to the 16th century' Editorial Comment: Page 9
'There was absolute silence... and sad
Full text Benedict XVI: I no longer have the strength to adequately fulfil my ministry
The media have misunderstood the Pope's comment
Argentines flock to Rio cathedral to meet Francis
Benedict XVI led us bravely through the abuse scandal
Conrad Black
Pope Bene was at hea true eco-
Mark Dowd
Thomas Carr Benedict's Protestant fans
Rachel Kelly The power of saving grace
CATHOLIC HERAL
Cardinal agle's ig test
Global refugee crisis offends God, says Pope
Catholics urged to 'reaffirm faith in common humanity'
Pope calls for end to Holy Land 'vortex of violence'
Cuba: Witness Hope Amid Despair
od's face

CHAPTER 4

"The Good and the Bad"

"Protestant firebrand Ian Paisley dies aged 88" was the headline under which the Associated Press (AP) carried news of his passing on 12th September 2014. At Vatican Radio, our news reader – the person who reads the news live to air – did what we'd trained him to do: checked the wires for the latest. I can't recall, now, whether the news reader read the headline live to air or not. If he gave it as he got it from the wires, then it was a good thing for us the news bulletin – mid-afternoon, if memory serves – was only going out as a local radio broadcast.

There was nothing wrong with the headline, mind. "It does exactly what it says on the tin" as the saying goes.

It was bad form – or would have been – for the Pope's (semi-) official broadcaster to be calling Paisley a firebrand, especially before he was in the ground or even cold. The news reader knew the technical part of his job and did it well. He was new in the job, though, and hadn't quite cottoned on to all the sensibilities and sensitivities of the peculiar kind of journalism we did in those days: official state journalism, which needed to account for certain diplomatic niceties, or else we'd get emails and sometimes phone calls from embassies, which would mostly give us occasion to chuckle, but occasionally brought a bit of grief.

I mention this because it is a way into an important lesson about how to read news you find in different kinds of news outlets. What you get from a given news outlet will depend largely on what the outlet – through its reporters and editors as well as its sources – knows about the story and about the institutional and cultural environment out of which the story comes. Indeed, what a news outlet knows about a story will often depend on how well they understand the institutions on which they are reporting and the cultural *milieux* in those institutions, as well as their own.

THERE IS NO "MSM"

The so-called "mainstream media" frequently come in for some harsh judgement and rough treatment from Catholics. Much of it is deserved, but not necessarily for the reasons those judgements and that treatment are given. Many people have noted for a very long time that "MSM" outlets tend to have an "anti-Catholic" bias. They accept the prevailing narrative about the Church – that she is "medieval" in outlook and design, benighted, "anti science" and "anti-[insert thing here]" – and are unwilling to learn. Some of those criticisms, I must say, hit the mark; sometimes, they're true. Often as not the inaccuracies – a favourite of mine is the talk one will frequently find about the Catholic Church's "abortion policy" – are the result of misunderstandings that Catholics are not terribly anxious to clarify.

Sometimes, MSM outlets go with the prevailing narrative because they don't have good religion reporters and journalists on staff, or because editors don't understand the way religion works – religion in general and Catholicism specifically – or because there's a deadline to meet and no time to spare on hashing out the minutiae for a story that doesn't appear to need it. Usually, it'll be a little from Column A, a little from Column B, and a little from Column C. It's not really important, most days, to know where the lion's share comes from. Most days, it's enough to be aware that, in all likelihood, the people reporting and editing the story just don't know what they're talking about as well as you'd like.

That doesn't mean there isn't a story. If *The Washington Post* tells you a bishop in West Virginia did very bad things, you can bet that there's a story worth knowing more about. That's what happened in the case of the former Bishop of

Wheeling-Charleston, Michael J Bransfield, who for thirteen years used the immense oil wealth bequeathed to his diocese to live in luxury, while getting up to all sorts of inappropriate behaviour with priests and seminarians. This was a story that *The Washington Post* told in painstaking, headline-grabbing detail.

What *The Washington Post* thinks of the Catholic Church's positions on abortion or gay marriage or anything else didn't matter then and doesn't now. They got the Bransfield story and did a great job reporting it. Catholic organisations might have done a better job with the technicalities, but then not as many people – not as many Catholics, even – would have read about it. More to the point, Catholic news organisations picked up the story and ran with it, filling in details and filling out blanks. They explained, through further reporting and analysis and commentary, what the story was about and why it was important to Catholics who care about the Church. In short, the system worked.

That's not to say the system couldn't have worked better than it did, or that it can't work better than it does. That doesn't mean the system's broken; not necessarily, anyway. It just means there's always room for improvement. We knew that already.

If the Catholic Church – by which I mean the whole body of the faithful, the People of God, not only or even primarily the clerical and hierarchical leadership – really wants to see better journalistic coverage of the Church, then what we need is a sort of Catholic "Spotlight" – or better – a Catholic *ProPublica*. In case you don't know what that is, *ProPublica* is an independent, non-profit investigative news organisation founded in 2007 and dedicated to exposing abuse of power and betrayal of public trust. They have more than a hundred journalists working on stories that have not only held powerful figures in government and business individually accountable, but directly contributed to legislative and policy reform.

"Investigative journalism requires a great deal of time and resources," *ProPublica* says in the "about" section of their website, and they're right. "Many newsrooms can no longer afford to take on this kind of deep-dive reporting", they note, again correctly. *ProPublica* gets most of their support from donations. "We are committed to uncovering the truth, no matter how long it takes or how much it costs, and we practice transparent financial reporting so donors know how their dollars are spent." Imagine that. No, really.

SETTING THE RECORD STRAIGHT

Here, a word is in order about how suspicion of motives and dislike for an organisation's editorial line can work all sorts of ill, not unlike the old Chinese folk tale about the fellow who misplaced his hammer in late autumn. Warren Horton Stuart tells a version of this story, which you'll find in William J Bennett's *Book of Virtues*. In that telling, it's an axe that has gone walkabout. Anyway, the fellow who'd lost the tool in the version I recall, had left it by the workbench on the side of the house facing his neighbour's place, and had seen his neighbour's boy mucking about in the side yard in the space between, and then rain came and then snow, and the hammer was gone, and all winter long, the neighbour's son looked more and more like the kind of boy who'd steal a hammer, until the spring came and the thaw and, lo and behold, there was the fellow's hammer sticking out of the mud. And the neighbour's son no longer looked like the kind of boy who'd steal a hammer.

The *National Catholic Reporter* was the first national Catholic newspaper in the United States to report on the clerical sexual abuse crisis. They picked up the story of Fr Gilbert Gauthe in Lafayette, Louisiana, and after that story had broken they stayed on it for years – nearly two full decades – until *Spotlight*. "They have it in for the Church!" people complained. "They're bad-mouthing our priests and bishops!" people said. The general idea was that the *Reporter* was either blowing things out of proportion, or using the abuse scandals to drive a doctrinally dubious "reform" agenda. Maybe, maybe not. The *Reporter* was right about the crisis of clerical sexual abuse and cover-up. In fact, the *Reporter* had only – barely – scratched the surface.

"Catholics on every side of every issue in the Church are perfectly aware of the bishops' corporate responsibility for the abuse crisis," I said in a short piece in the *Catholic Herald* on 28th July 2018. That was the day Pope Francis took away Uncle Ted McCarrick's red hat. The piece turned out to be something of a mission statement for me. I noted that people were "rightly appalled by [the bishops'] haste to plead ignorance and pretend responsibility only lies with the 'few' who did the evil." I went on to say that the bishops – though they had been lions in other fights – were goats in this one, to a man:

> Nevertheless, many of us are too quick to blame the prelates on the other side of the ideological divide. That temptation will prove fatal to any reform effort. Catholics must resist it. Bishops who have been our allies and standard-bearers – sometimes even our heroes – in other situations may turn out to fail us in this one. In fact, they already have.
>
> Said differently, we can use this crisis as a proxy in our ideological battles, or we can fight this fight together, ruthlessly and without stint, until we have won; we cannot do both. If we choose the first path, we shall make ourselves the evildoers' accomplices. The second path is the only one that offers hope. But it will also require us to smash our own idols.

I daresay the events of the intervening three years have largely borne me out. I'd be lying if I said I hate being right but I would have been happy to have seen myself proven wrong. I mean about the bishops, and also about us. We need to find our hammers and remember how to use them.

None of that is to say that the MSM are impeccable, above reproach, beyond suspicion, or purely motivated. If an MSM organisation tells you the Pope changed doctrine, for example, it's a safe bet things are either more or less… complicated. The *Post* likely has the goods – even if they don't understand what they have or how things turned out as well as one should like – but the doctrine story is almost certainly wrong. Here's a tale out of school to illustrate the point.

This is another story about another time some AP copy popped up on the wires, and a news reader assumed it to be correct. "Pope Benedict XVI has reversed centuries of traditional Roman Catholic teaching on limbo," the story breathlessly announced, "approving a Vatican report released Friday that says there were 'serious' grounds to hope that children who die without being baptised can go to heaven." He hadn't. All he'd done was receive a report from the International Theological Commission.

The ITC study did say the thing the AP said it said, but Pope Benedict hadn't done the thing the AP said he'd done. People wanted the AP's version of the story to be true – limbo is a much misunderstood theological idea, both within and without the Church – and "Pope changes doctrine" makes a better story lead than "Pope receives wonky white paper from theological talking shop" so there you have it. It's worth mentioning here that reporters almost never write their own headlines and frequently don't write their own lede lines.

So, if your first question was, "Why didn't the reporter get it right?" the answer may well be that the reporter isn't the one who got it wrong.

This sort of thing happens all the time. If you read the news, you'll notice it happening without noticing yourself noticing it, especially if you've come to expect MSM outlets to get it wrong. Sometimes, it will be the sort of thing that gets under one's skin. Usually, we go right on. It's the sort of thing that has become part of the environment.

KNOWING "ENOUGH"

The thing to remember about the MSM is that they can be very useful sources of information, if you know how to use them. If you see a story about the Pope cancelling limbo, you can wonder what it's really about. You may get a general idea from the MSM story, but if you're a serious Catholic, it won't be enough to tell you what's really going on. These days, the internet makes it much easier than it used to be to get the story straight from the source. The ITC report, for example, was available on the Vatican website. The non-Catholic, for whom the story was written, may have gone away from the AP story thinking one thing when the reality was another, but he or she had read an interesting story about the Church and probably hadn't even noticed most of the inaccuracies that annoyed Catholics, let alone noticed him- or herself noticing.

CHAPTER 5

What Have We Learned?

One of the distinctions I find myself frequently at pains to make is that between scandal and crisis. Scandals come and go. They are the thing of a day – maybe a few days, or a few months – and then we're on to the next thing. Whether the next thing is another scandal is beside the point, for now. It may be – and it may be somehow related to the last one – but it need not be, and deserves treatment on its own terms and merits, whatever its relation to the last thing. Crises, on the other hand, are rather persistent, even if they have moments of acute manifestation. They frequently remain hidden from view for years or even decades.

The leadership crisis in the Church is an example. It's something that has been around for a good, long while. It is rooted in the mystery of sin itself, and at bottom is a spiritual disease. I've said elsewhere that I agree with Pope Francis's diagnosis of the sickness as caused by lust for power – *libido dominandi* – which warps everything it touches and is always ready to use whatever warped parts it finds along the way. The scandals are an effect of the crisis, not a cause.

The crisis in the Church will be with us for the foreseeable future. Don't take my word for it. "This will not be over in our lifetime," said Fr Hans Zollner SJ, the young German Jesuit who runs the Pontifical Gregorian University's Centre for Child Protection, "at least in countries where they have not yet started to talk about it." He was speaking to participants in an international conference at Fordham University in New York, in March 2018. The crisis, in other words, is a fixture of Catholic life now, and it is going to get worse before it gets better.

Fr Zollner was speaking specifically about the crisis of clerical sexual abuse and cover-up. That's not the only manifestation of the leadership crisis. It's important for people to know about what's going on in the Church generally. It's important for Catholics and other Christians to know what's going on, because we have a stake in it. It's important for others to know what's going on in the Church, because the Church is public and they have a right to the gospel she exists to make credible.

A while back, I quoted John Adams to the effect that citizens have a right to know about the characters and conduct of their rulers. It's interesting to note that Adams considered the Catholic Church an enemy of political liberty. Sometimes, maybe – and we hope he had better reason to believe that in his day than we do to believe it in ours – but, here's the thing: the Church is a polity – a *societas perfecta* as we used to say, a "perfect society" – by which we mean that she has all the powers to order lives and regulate conduct necessary and conducive to a flourishing human community.

Whatever else that means – it would need several volumes the length of this one to unpack – it means that the right to knowledge of the character and conduct of rulers inheres in each and every member of the baptised faithful.

That is why it is important for Catholics to keep abreast of the doings in the Church – whether at the centre of power here in Rome or in their home dioceses and countries – and that's where journalism comes in.

Every Catholic is a part of this story – every person is a part of it, like it or not, know it or not – and we all need to do our best.

The journalist tells the story as it unfolds. The responsibility of the Catholic journalist is the same as that of the journalist *sic et simpliciter*, but the Catholic journalist's heuristic instruments and general tool set are different. As JD Flynn put it last year, in his preface to my book on the crisis:

> The Catholic journalist has an odd task. He must, on the one hand, approach his subject using the tools of his profession: seeking objectivity and fairness in his work. He must be willing to recognise the Church's successes and failures on a human level, and the abilities and deficiencies of her leaders. On the other hand, he has to remember that the tools of his profession cannot, by themselves, tell the whole story of the Church – that they cannot unpack the movement of the Holy Spirit, the manifestation of Divine Providence.

In the afterword to that book, I noted that the Catholic journalist's professional responsibility always overlaps to some extent with the commitments every baptised member of the faithful has undertaken, but isn't identical or exactly co-extensive with them. The journalist's questions are those anyone and everyone has – or would have, with just a little knowledge of any given situation – and the journalist's job is threefold: to know enough to know what the questions are; to frame the questions in a way that comports with known facts and admits of answer; then, to get the answers as fully as possible, and tell people.

What about Catholic readers of journalism? All through this book, I've toggled back and forth between the twin perspectives of the people who produce the news and the people who consume it. Now, I'd like to focus more closely on how to read the news without becoming unhinged. I'll pull together the things we've talked about already.

If most people for most of human history didn't know who the Pope was, then what's happening in Rome today isn't likely to make a world-shaking difference to most of our daily lives. It isn't that history isn't happening right now; the point is that history is always happening. I'm glad we have a chance to know a little more about what's happening in Rome or in the local chancery. That said, the truths of the faith are rock solid, and the duties of Christians to their fellows don't change with the comings and goings of popes and cardinals.

Remember, too, that big headlines and sensational claims don't make a story important. They're what journalistic outlets use to sell the news. In order to understand a story – to get a feel for what's there and what's not – you need to read critically.

Is this story telling me something I need to know? Even if it is, does it play to my worries, concerns, fears, misgivings about this or that set of people? Does it tell me about bad stuff people did, and are the alleged perpetrators of these misdeeds the sort of people about whom – on a bad day – I want to think bad things? Did the story tell me they were bad people, or just show me what they did? Whose story is it? Am I reading original reporting? Does the evidence adduced establish the facts of the case? Who wrote this? Who published it? Have they been right before? Have they been badly wrong? What do they know about the general field or institution or culture in which the story is situated?

Not every story will require you to ask all those questions. Some stories won't require you to ask any of them. Getting in the habit of asking them will help you develop a "feel" for the news you encounter.

KNOWING WHAT YOU KNOW

Here, we've seen a little about how the truths of the faith can help us stay grounded. Whether it's a claim about the Pope not being the Pope, or a claim about the Pope teaching heresy, or a claim about the Pope being a Socialist or a Nazi or a Freemason or an alien (yes, that one is out there), know in your bones that the Barque of Peter will not founder. True or not, stories repeating those claims aren't trying to inform you, except incidentally. Whenever you see a story purporting to show you the proof that there is a massive conspiracy to seat a pope who will change Church teaching and inaugurate the age of the anti-Church, chances are it's time to read something else.

We noted earlier that we are promised – by a hope which cannot disappoint – that the Barque of Peter will come safely to port. We also noted that we've no guarantee what shape she'll be in when she does call. If a ship is – or appears to be – headed for the shoals, it is easy to get worked up. Sometimes, it will be necessary to raise the alarm, even knowing what we know.

"The Pope's a prince, isn't he?" says the Duke of Norfolk to Thomas More in Robert Bolt's *A Man for All Seasons*.

"He is", Bolt's More replies. "And a bad one?" asks Norfolk. "Bad enough", says More, "but the theory is that he is also the Vicar of God, the descendant of St Peter, our only link with Christ." Norfolk says it is "a tenuous link." More replies, "Oh, tenuous, indeed."

PARTIALITY IS INEVITABLE

You'll sometimes hear talk of how "impartiality" should be a characteristic of news reporting. In the sense that reporters shouldn't take sides, it's generally true. Neither should readers of news. Earlier, we also discussed a little about how news stories are always "partial" accounts. They can't tell the whole story – certainly not in one go – even when the story is an investigative report running several thousand words in length.

The best reporters will give you a snapshot of a situation. They'll describe it well. They'll also tell you what they are describing, and they'll be forthright about what the facts they report mean and what they don't – what they prove, what they indicate may be the case, and what they rule out – and readers should be looking for those sorts of things in the news stories they read.

Does the reporter have sources with direct knowledge of pertinent matters and are those sources on the record? If not, why not? Did the reporter go to the other side for comment? If there are allegations of misconduct or other wrongdoing, what is the evidence? Is there a denial? How much space did the subject(s) get? Those are some of the things for which to look, when you are reading news reports.

When you are reading news analysis, the first thing to ascertain is whether what you're reading really is news analysis, or whether it is commentary. The best analysts explain general political, social, and cultural dynamics at work in a given story, so that "what it means" can begin to come into focus. The best analysts do two things: explain complex news stories in terms accessible to readers and explain how – and why – stories that appear either straightforward or straightforwardly controversial really aren't. They're good at what they do because they know the players and the field. That makes them capable of understanding the complex interplay of personality, perception, political reality, and interests – real and perceived – that make up the dynamics of every place where decisions are made.

Analysis can be fun. It can convey real insight about weighty matters in ways that delight readers by showing them things in new and different lights. Analysis can also cast shadow – even throw shade – on popular decisions, or gently remind readers that there is a downside to that thing that everyone thinks is great. In other words, news analysis is what reporters write when they want to show a little of their personality and share their cast of mind with their readers, and shed light on what decision-makers think and how decision-makers think about it. That's what readers should be looking for in news analysis.

COMMENTARY IS CHEAP (WE NEED LOTS OF IT)

The heading for this section is the first half of an old journalistic maxim, which continues with "Reporting is expensive." Part of the reason we say commentary is cheap is that "Everybody has a take." It's easy to get someone to write about this or that on-going topic.

Newspapers and magazines build readership and an institutional identity in part by commissioning well-written commentary and opening their opinion pages to people with strong opinions who write with distinctive style. I think that magazines, especially, best serve their readers by giving them a broad range of opinions – by letting them hear the best each side has to offer – and letting the readers make up their minds. This will mean that readers will come across things with which they disagree fairly regularly in any publication with a strong commentary section or focus. The publication owes readers good, thoughtful writing on genuinely interesting – not merely curious – subjects. Readers, in my experience, are more than happy to engage a piece by a writer whose opinions the reader does not share. Maybe the reader finds them abhorrent; that's what Letters to the Editor are for.

This way of thinking about commentary – an absolutely essential part of the full-service journal, be it a print daily, weekly, monthly, or online publication – is not as prevalent as it was when I was starting out. Many readers balk at anything that doesn't wave the right flag with sufficient vim and vigour, and are outraged – outraged! – by any sort of contrary take on all manner of opinable question. I'm not talking about pieces platforming dissent from established teaching, or outlandish political opinion, or apology for moral turpitude. I'm talking about things that are well within the bounds of reasonable discourse.

I hope this will change, and soon. We already know what the people with whom we agree are thinking. We all need to know what the people with whom we disagree are thinking, too. It's just part of being informed.

THE GOOD, THE BAD, THE UGLY

Earlier, I gave my elevator pitch for more investigative and long-form journalism, especially in and for the Church. Part of the reason I believe we need more of that is that it's the way we get the kind of reform we need. That's only part of it – the "bad news" part. Here's the good news part of it.

Telling people that things are rosy when they're not is just plain wrong. Showing them Christians doing the work of the Gospel in circumstances at least as trying as their own is of the essence, especially given the mess we're in just now. While I know that the kinds of trouble on which I make my living will abound, I can't now think of anyone in my trade who wouldn't jump at the chance to have funding for in-depth research on people and issues close to home and on-the-ground reportage from around the world, on stories of the Church punching way above her weight.

WHAT READERS CAN DO

If I'm right about this, then readers are hungry, starved even: for reportage that really informs; for analysis that illustrates dynamics by illuminating decision-makers' cast(s) of mind and hierarchies of goods while making structures of power transparent; for commentary characterised by genuine independence and candour of mind. They need it – we need it – but have almost forgotten what it even looks or sounds like, and need to reacquire the taste for it, too. You'll hear a good deal of talk about the need to overcome the polarisation of the public square, but very few people are really doing anything about it.

I've said what I'm about to say elsewhere – in lots of different places, in slightly different ways according to the occasion, the public for whom I was writing, and the circumstances about which I was writing – but here are two things readers can do:

- Keep in mind that being Catholic means participating in an intellectual tradition that has always prized the work of making subtle and particular distinctions within the unity of truth. When we're at our best, we encourage each other to seek – and always to be in awe of – the infinite nuance necessary and possible within the oneness of knowledge. We're confident in a way that comes from knowing that the world is a big place, the Church true, and God better than we are.

- Remember that Catholic faith requires us to think all the good we can of those with whom we disagree, and to work for an increase of our capacity for thinking well. Again, that's not to say we ought to try to think the good we can't. Sometimes, people do bad things. Sometimes, the bad things they do are our business.

Even when we are all at our very best – and when does that ever happen? – we are imperfect creatures. Some are more imperfect than others, certainly, but all of us need a good bit of work. The world is fallen. We await fullness of its redemption. We have good days and bad – and there have been some big wins along the way – but the only true and lasting victory belongs to Christ, Our Lord, who conquered sin and death. Most of what we do is muddling – I've said this before, too – and that's all the more reason to get on with it.

IMAGE CREDITS

Cover: montage featuring headlines from *The Catholic Herald*. Photo of St Peter's Basilica, Rome, Italy © Tomas1111/Dreamstime.com.

Page 6: © Andrea Sabbadini/Alamy Stock Photo

Page 15: Pope Pius XI., Guglielmo Marconi and Eugenio Pacelli, at the inauguration of the Vatican Radio, 1931. © Sueddeutsche Zeitung Photo/ Alamy Stock Photo.

Page 20: © François Lochon/Gamma-Rapho via Getty Images.

Page 28: *Christ Giving the Keys to St. Peter* by Pietro Perugino. Wikimedia Commons CC0 License.

Dreamstime.com: page 7: © Waltercicchetti; p.12 © Miruna Iancu; p.13 © Wellphotos; p.32: © Ievgen Gomeniuk; p.33: © Cat Moon; p.40: © Piyamas Dulmunsumphun; p.54: © Martin Molcan; p.55: © Damianpalus; p.73: © Shopartgallerycom; p.82: © Blurf; p.83: © Rinofelino.